IOD27076

Stories of
Loss and Survival

by
Michelle Oleff Cohn

**Heartprint Boxes
Publications**

**Vanderblumen Publications
La Mesa, California**

Special Thank You

I want to thank all the people that have contributed to this book. All those who unselfishly gave their stories did so entirely to help and give hope to others. This book would have never happened without the contributions of these very kind people.

I also want to give a very special thank you to Arlene Pollard, L.C.S.W. and Dr. Ken Druck who gave their time, thoughts, and answers to all my questions.

Dedication

 I would like to dedicate this book to Dani and Maxx. You are my hopes, my thoughts, my wishes, my dreams, and my heart! I love you!

Oleff Cohn, Michelle
    Stories of Loss and Survival

Softcover
ISBN 978-0-982-9909-0-2(pbk.)

Printed in the United States of America

Table Of Contents

"Grief knits two hearts in closer bonds than happiness ever can; and common sufferings are far stronger links than common joys."

-Alphonse de Lamartine

CHAPTER 1
INTRODUCTION

I wanted to write this book after going through the experience of a personal loss, and not knowing what to do with myself. It seemed like such a blur at the beginning, and then when all the chaos was over, I was left with loneliness. I often thought, what do I do now? How am I supposed to go back to normal life? I didn't want to. I couldn't focus on anything. I didn't want to be around celebrations. I just wanted to crawl into my bed and sleep until I felt better. I discovered that going to bed and sleeping did not seem to be the answer either. I often wondered, what do I do with myself?

Many people called me to give their support. As much as I appreciated it, I did not feel that they understood what I was really feeling. I just did not know what to do with myself. It seemed the only thing distracting my pain temporarily, was hearing about others who had gone through a loss and seemed to be functioning now. I wanted to hear how they got through their pain and whether it was ever going to be better for me. Would I ever smile or laugh again? The stories helped me in knowing I was not alone.

Society doesn't know what to do with grief. There is no known cure, magical treatment, or one answer as to when someone will feel better again. It's just hopeful to know others have been through it and survived. I wanted and needed to know how! I needed some kind of hope that I could cling on to. Unfortunately, there is no one answer, no magical pill, and no cure.

This is a process that **you** have to go through at **your** own pace, **your** own way. My father-in-law, who has lost two children and several other family members in his lifetime, is often asked by others going through a loss, "when will I feel better?" His answer is always the same.

He says, "the love, connection and affection you feel for the person you lost, is equal to the pain and suffering that you will go through." He explains that he has been through several losses, but the loss of the people he has had the closest connection with, are the ones he continues to mourn.

"Those are the ones that just never go away," he continues. "It does get easier with time, but there is always a void for that person." He also stated how he has a very difficult time with people who have been through the loss of a child because sometimes people say to him, "I understand what you're going through."

Although they mean well, no one understands the feelings that **you** are going through. It is **your** loss. It was **your** relationship, **your** connection. No one can tell you that they understand.

What this book offers are stories of others who have been through a devastating loss and survived. There are many stories of different types of losses. The common denominator is the pain. They all handled it in their own way, in their own time. They agreed to share their stories to help and give comfort to others.

This book also contains suggestions of how to help you on your process through grief. The ideas presented have come from people who have written stories in this book, counselors and experts that I have talked with, as well as a combination of many books and articles I have read.

You will find the resources and websites at the end of this book for further guidance. I hope they can offer many more suggestions, thoughts and ideas for help with healing and survival.

CHAPTER 2
LOSS OF A GRANDPARENT

One day they're with you, the next day they're gone. Why does life do this, it just seems so wrong.

The person you loved is with you no more. It pains you deep inside, right down to your core.

Nothing you do will bring them back to life. You must accept the painful truth without putting up a fight.

So how do you move forward while you are in such great pain?

It's so hard when you're feeling that nothing is the same.

Inhale strong, take a deep breath, and try hard to understand.

Listen to the wise words from others, and accept each helping hand.

Don't give up when you feel that you're almost at the end. So many people love you deeply, and will be there as your friend.

Stay focused on the good, and what you learned from your loved one.

Take it one day at a time, and the healing will soon come.

Remember it is only the body that is gone, not the spirit inside. The body was only the vessel for the sprit to reside.

It is now your turn to carry on the love and wisdom that was shared.

Hold the memories close, and accept that it's okay to be scared.

Each day that you continue to move forward will be another victory.

Although it doesn't seem like it, one day you will be free.

Forgetting is not an option; hold your loved one deep inside.

Through you they will live on, from that you cannot hide.

Allow yourself to feel the hurt; the loss is so much to bear.

The pain that is felt inside you simply shows how much you care.

As hard as it is pick your head up, and make it one more day.

Your loved ones will forever live inside you, for their essence is here to stay!

CHAPTER 3
LOSS OF A MOTHER

Dealing with the loss of our mother, began approximately ten years prior to her actual passing. Our mother, Paulette Crivello, was diagnosed with Pick's Disease at the age of fifty. For five years prior to that, the doctors thought she had early stages of Alzheimer's disease. However, the characteristics of Alzheimer's did not fit with our mother's age and actions.

Instead, Pick's Disease is a form of dementia that affects the frontal lobe of the brain, which controls the cognitive and behavioral process of your body. The most frustrating aspect of the disease is not knowing the cause of her illness.

Over a time span of fifteen years, we had to watch our mother change from an independent, strong, vibrant, and social woman to one who was no longer able to communicate, walk, feed herself, and carry out daily hygiene routines, such as the simple tasks that we all take for granted. Watching this take place was the hardest thing we ever had to endure.

My family dealt with so many emotions; ranging from sadness to anger, knowing that she had no control over her actions. We all found comfort in humor and laughter, especially when our children were around. If we were able to make light of an odd or embarrassing behavior, it made the reality of slowly losing our mother a little less painful.

With any terminal illness, you can't help but wonder, how long must we watch her deteriorate before our eyes? When the doctors notified our family that she had approximately five years to live, it became more of a relief than a surprise.

Over time, we prepared ourselves for the day when we must truly say goodbye. Most people don't get that opportunity. We found more comfort in the knowing, and making sure that we spent extra time with her in her final days.

Our mother caught a cold during Christmas of 2006 at the age of sixty. She was so weak and frail at this point that this cold ultimately was the cause of her passing. Upon taking her to see her doctor, they advised my father to seek hospice care for her. Hospice took care of her in our home for the next five days. This was the only time that our father let someone else help with her care. He was her sole care giver since her first behavioral change occurred.

As my mother laid there in her hospital bed in our family room, we kept watch over her day and night. We reminisced about the days when our mom was well. How she was the life of the party and always involved at our school and in our lives.

Michelle Oleff Cohn

Once we told her to stop holding on for us, and that we would all be okay, she knew it was time to let go. She passed away on January 14, 2007, with her family at her bedside.

Nothing can prepare you for their final breath of life. Knowing that you will never see them again is the hardest thing to accept. So many years, that she will not be experiencing with us and her grandchildren, still brings us much sadness. A day does not go by that we don't think of her, but our lives have been forever changed by this experience. Our hearts go out to families currently dealing with a loved one with Pick's disease.

Following our family's devastation came the need to bring awareness to the world that this disease exists, and that people all over the world are misdiagnosed. Our family would like anyone who thinks their loved one is suffering from Pick's to contact The Association for Frontotemporal Dementias at www.ftd-picks.org.

By Lisa Crivello-Hudnall and

Lori Crivello-Taranto

CHAPTER 4
LOSS OF AN UNCLE

On January 23, 2006, a father, brother, uncle, and child died of Leukemia cancer. Bob Johnson was forty-seven years old and I was eleven years old. I remember the day he was diagnosed, the day he died, the last time I saw him and exactly where I was when I found out.

During the summer, I was staying at my grandma's house on my dad's side of the family. I came out of the small room by the family room after watching some television. Mummi, my grandma, had just hung up the phone with a concerned look on her face. I sat near my grandpa, Poppi.

A little teary-eyed Mummi said, "Uncle Bob been diagnosed with Leukemia cancer."

I instantly began crying and I had no idea why. I didn't even know the meaning of Leukemia. I didn't know people died from leukemia. I didn't think my uncle and godfather had a disease. There was little I understood about cancer, but I felt stupid asking what it was because everyone seemed to know and was obviously upset about it.

Through the weeks that followed, I slowly learned more about Leukemia and how deadly it was. For months, my day would consist of school, homework, and then driving to the hospital to play monopoly with all my cousins in the waiting room.

Sometimes my dad, or aunt would go inside Uncle Bob's room but I personally never went. I was too afraid to go in. It's a scary place, a hospital, so many tubes and needles. I was too afraid of the unknown and what would happen when I saw him.

Would I cry or would I forget how to speak? I was supposed to be strong like the rest of the family. However, I did draw him pictures that I can barely remember. They were pictures of his favorite place, ocean and pictures of animals, and I had hoped he would live.

Being a typical fifth grader, I wanted to make lemonade stand and raise money for his cause because in my mind there was no chance of him dying. I was told that it could happen, but I thought it never would.

Finally, I was told that Uncle Bob could remain at home for a month. During that time I only stopped by once. When I walked into the house, I saw my uncle, but he seemed like a stranger. I had forgotten how to act around him and I had forgotten how he acted around me.

So I was quiet and shy. I awkwardly gave him a hug when saying goodbye and said all of two words to him. But he wasn't like that. He was happy. His smile made his cheeks like two big red plums and his chuckle was joyful.

"Hey, Emma!" he said as I walked through the door. He was grateful for everything and grateful to be back at home. Out of everything, I regret acting that way the most because that was the last time I saw uncle Bob.

Time passed and as I coming home from my usual fifth grade day, my mom had picked me up from school and as usual I sat down at the dining room table to do my homework. Sometime before dark, my mom called to me, "Emma." By the sound of her voice I thought I was in trouble.

As I walked down the hall, I thought of anything I could have done wrong. When I got to her room, she plopped me on top of her bed with the fluffy white comforter.

"I must have done something really bad this time," I thought as she looked at me with concern.

"Uncle Bob died sweetie," she said out of nowhere it seemed.

I wasn't prepared for her to say **THAT**! I thought, under no circumstances was I emotionally prepared to hear those words. I had never thought my uncle would die. With a disease like cancer, adults prepare themselves for the emotional roller coaster. Children have so much hope, there was little thought of my uncle dying during that time. I was determined to make him survive. I didn't believe or realize that he could have actually died.

In my mind, I **KNEW** he would survive. Those were my thoughts through everything. I did not prepare myself for that moment or those words because I was too young to understand reality. It was like all that hope was crushed under death's shoes.

I cried the moment she told me as you're supposed to, but I cried more because I was supposed to cry not because I was automatically hit with sadness. It hadn't even hit me that he was actually gone. It seemed like he had just gone on vacation and would be back home soon.

In fact, I went to school the next day and easily told my best friend that my uncle had just died the night before. I went on for weeks like this.

My dad and I spoke nothing of Uncle Bob's passing except for the funeral date. It wasn't until I went to the funeral that I sincerely cried for the death of my uncle.

While sitting in the fourth row back next to my older cousin, I cried harder than I had ever cried, harder than when I fell off my bike, harder than when I wasn't allowed to go to my friend's birthday party, and even harder than when I was forced to leave my school of nine years and leave my best friends.

I cried because as I was sitting in the fourth row seeing a casket, and in that casket was a dead body, who was my uncle. This was my uncle that I had looked up to for years, who had taken me to the beach to play in the sand. This was the same uncle that would never again be at family birthdays, Christmas, Thanksgiving, and Easter. Never again would I touch, hear, or see my uncle Bob. I cried mostly not because of my pain, but because of his pain.

After months in the hospital enduring chemotherapy and other brutal treatments and after years and years of happiness, to have his last moments spent in a cold white room with one window and a small television. I cried because he would no longer go to the beach, see his children, nieces and nephews. He would never again see his siblings and parents and that all his hard work would be for nothing.

It took me years to realize that he died for a reason. He died to escape the pain. He lived his life surrounded by people who loved him.

Unfortunately, he was put through the pain of treatments and hospitals, and the pain of watching his family mourn over his sickness. By his dying, he was no longer put through such pain, he no longer needed to be away from his family or in a hospital bed with medications all around him. He no longer needed to feel weak and sick. I feel that now after his death he is happier than he was the couple months before he died.

Years later, it's still hard to tell people the whole story. In fact, I don't really tell anyone. I think about him often and remind myself how much happier he must be. I have also accepted the fact that I will never see his smile again, or hear his laugh or his peaceful words. However, I will never accept him being forgotten, but I know forgetting him won't be a problem. Rest in peace Robert Johnson.

By Emma Johnson

15 years old

CHAPTER 5
LOSS OF A BELOVED PET

She walked into my life as if she owned my world. A rescue not more than a year old with all the spunk of a tiger. As the months passed by, I learned she was special. Her thoughts anticipated my every emotion and thought.

It was just a year later that the cat parade occurred when Sir Charles arrived at the door. Following Missy into her now secure home, Missy looked up at me as if to say, "Can I keep him?" I looked down at the 20-pound five-year-old cat, ladened with battle scars from cat fights, overwhelmed with fleas and probably harboring worms. Her eyes told me to keep him, so a visit to the vet's office and a bath cleared up any hesitation I might have had about keeping him.

As the years now passed, the two became inseparable and so much a part of my life that I woke each morning to find them on either side of my bed awaiting their next meal and the chance to follow me around the home. Our morning chats were amusing as each of us had something quite profound to say.

As the last part of the year was quickly approaching, I began to notice Missy's heart rate was racing and she was panting as if to catch her breath. It was a cold morning and Missy had not arrived in the kitchen as she usually did each morning guiding the way for Sir Charles to eat.

I heard a scream from the bedroom and found her panting under the bed. Her back legs had given out and she was crying for help. As I scooped her into my arms and raced out the door to the vet's office, I knew something terrible had gone wrong. My strong brave cat was dying. As we drove to the vet's office, I heard her purring then silence. We arrived at the door of the vet's with Missy in my arms asking for help. She took her last breath and was silent. She was gone in less than one half hour.

I was stunned to think she was gone. I cried and left the vet's office after making arrangements for her burial.

That night I cried with such intensity that Sir Charles knew something was very wrong. He searched the house for Missy thinking I would have brought her home.

As the days passed, we both mourned her death. The loss and pain ease with each passing day.

Then when all else appeared empty, a new litter of kittens was found on the property of a friend. Another rescue litter had been born and I hesitated to take one, but the feeling that this was the time was so strong I agreed.

Home I sped with a small eight-week-old kitten. Sir Charles was confused when I placed the small creature next to him. Sir Charles snarled and growled, but did not hurt the little one. Prince Harry as he would be called stood his ground. He walked right up to Sir Charles and licked him on the nose. Sir Charles was stunned. He did not know what to make of this. It has been just four months since Prince Harry has been with us. As the days pass, he has become a major part of our lives and has helped to heal the hurt of the loss of Missy.

For those of you who don't believe in miracles, I swear it is Missy's spirit in this little kitten come back to continue the journey of life with us.

By Glenna A. Bloemen
La Mesa, California

January, 2012

CHAPTER 6
LOSS OF A FATHER

*"Expect trouble as an inevitable part of life and repeat to yourself, the most comforting words of all.
This, too, shall pass."*

-Ann Landers

I remember the exact moment when I said to my dad in tears, "please don't die before me."

No, I was not six years old. I wasn't even 12. I was a 21-year-old college student.

Was it a premonition? Was it a warning from God of what was to come?

Fast forward my story to August 5, 1991. For some sentimental reason, I decided to come home from college and stay with my parents for the summer. It was a Monday morning and when I woke up, I was surprised to find my hard working dad at home. When I asked him why he wasn't at work his answer was simple, "It's a beautiful day."

We had breakfast together and then he walked me to my car. I left for work and I vividly remember looking in my rearview mirror as he waved to me until I was out if sight.

Stories of Loss and Survivial

At 3:00 p.m., I looked at my watch and thought about calling my dad to see how his "beautiful day" was going. A customer asked for my help and I was never able to make that call.

With the store closing at 9:00 p.m., I decided to take my last break at 8 o'clock. After resting for a minute or two, a woman in a business suit stuck her face in the break room.

"Are you Michelle? Will you come with me?"

What was going on? Was I being fired? Promoted?

As I followed the woman into a small office, she asked me to sit down. She sat across from me and quietly, sweetly, told me there had been an emergency and some family members were waiting to see me. In walked two of my cousins and my aunt, arms wrapped around each other for support and comfort.

My cousin, the nurse, held back her tears as best she could to say, "There was an accident. It's your dad. He passed away."

I'm not sure what happened next, but I remember being in the car as they drove me home. This is my worst nightmare coming true. Why? Out of all the people in the world, why him? My best friend, my mentor, my support and cheer leader, my mechanic, my comedian, my doctor, my spiritual leader.....the list goes on and on.

When we arrived at home, our street looked like a parking lot.

My bright future was reduced to crying myself to sleep only to awaken to the horrific reality that he was gone. The phone kept ringing. The florists kept coming. There were so many people in our home. I did not want to talk to anyone because that would solidify something I didn't want to face; life without my dad.

When would he walk through the door? When would he call? In my dreams he was alive.

The memorial service was at our family church where my dad sang in the choir, served on the building committee, and probably did more than I will ever know.

It was standing room only, and people had to stand outside to listen to the music and eulogies from the speakers. It seemed as if all eyes were on me. I'm sure my sister and mom felt the same way. I was completely depleted; mentally, emotionally, and physically. I was numb. I had shut down and could do little more then sit, stand, walk, and eat whatever was forced in to my mouth.

Thinking back, I felt as if I had tunnel vision. I could see what was before me, but the peripherals were black. I knew that I would die soon, as well.

I shook my head when I realized that happened 18-1/2 years ago. I do believe that "time heals all wounds", but it doesn't take away the scars. My scars are so huge that I am not the same person I was before my dad passed away. I was forever changed.

For so many months, days, minutes, I begged God to comfort me. He gave me peace. I felt orphaned, but God was my strength. It was just God and I now and 18 years later, he is still there with me.

I began to come out of myself imposed cave where I felt like a little girl curled up in the dark. My relatives opened their arms to me when my mom escaped to the comfort of her parents in another state and my sister retreated to the sanctuary and safety of the camp where she worked and lived.

I began to let people love me and take care of me. Looking back I realized I had become so dependent upon others to take care of me, my health, my shelter and my future.

Collectively, my extended family encouraged me to return to college and I graduated. There I reconnected with my home away from home. I met new friends and leaned on old ones.

One professor, in particular, reached out to me and gave me mini therapy sessions as we'd walk from his class to my next class. I believe he was "heaven sent". So many people would either tell me they didn't know what to say to me, or they'd say "he's in a better place." At the time, that gave me zero comfort. My professor understood. He gave me time to talk, he listened, he advised, he cared.

I felt the best when I could talk openly and freely without someone saying that the topic made them feel uncomfortable. The loss never goes away. It's as if your heart has a permanent hole in it that can never be filled.

Time goes on, and you begin to adjust to life without your loved one. It's scary, but you have to go on. You will go on. I'm living proof.

By Michelle Arthur

CHAPTER 7
LOSS OF A FRIEND

*"The healthy and stong individual is the one
who asks for help when he needs it. Whether he's
got an abcess on his knee or in his soul."*

-Rona Barrett

When I was little, my mom used to tell me that whenever someone died, they became a star. So when anyone close to us passed away, I would try to find them in the sky.

Death is an ending, but it is not an answer. It brings infinite questions that always seemed unanswerable to me. But the death of one person gave me the answers I never thought existed.

Lucas Stover was not a name you would forget. He was not a face you couldn't remember. He was not someone that merely blended in with everyone else. He was different from everyone. If people were colors, he was his own; one that no one could recreate or copy. He had the capability to do something that seems extremely simple, but I've come to realize not many people know how to do; listen.

When someone wants to make you feel better, they try and give you advice or tell you everything's going to be okay. But he never did that. He wouldn't promise things were going to be all right because he didn't know if they would be. He didn't try to explain something he didn't understand. He would open his arms and quiet your cries with a hug and an open ear. He never said a word. He would listen to whatever anyone had to say and just nod his head.

He was everyone's shoulder to cry on; it would seem a blessing and a curse to most people. But to Lucas, he knew that just by letting someone lean on him, he was sharing their pain. He was lifting a weight of whatever significance off someone's shoulders.

That's what I miss the most about him. Being able to call him, crying. He would say nothing but I never felt alone. I always knew he was there, even if I couldn't hear him talking. The realization of this allowed me to discover two answers that I will carry with me forever.

The tragedy of death is selfish. When someone dies, we grieve because the place they filled in our lives is suddenly empty. It's a change we're simply not ready for.

We're horrified by the reality of never seeing someone again. And while this is tragic, it is self-centered. Death is about who it takes away, not the people it takes them from. Especially in a young death, it is truly tragic because they didn't get to receive a future or reach their true potential. And from this, I found my second answer.

Death should not be significant. It is a test of our reactions. In his goodbye letter, the most important thing Lucas wrote to me was, "Our reactions make us who we are. Trying to change them, hide them, or question them is bottling your pain and burying it in a place you can't hide from but where no one else can find them."

Death is an unknown end. But a final goodbye should not change the effect someone had in your life. Darkness should not dispute the fact that there was once light.

Lucas was a distinct fire in my life and his death did not extinguish it. Now, it's up to me to decide how to keep the fire alive. And thanks to my mom, I know exactly how.

Lucas is a star I try to find every night. And if I ever need someone to lean on, I know the sky is listening.

On October 26th, 2009, I woke up at 3:42 a.m. to see that I had two missed calls. One was from my best friend, Lucas; and the other was his mother calling me to tell me that he was dead. I'm not going to spin a colorful story or try to hide what he did. His mother went into his room to check on him, as she had done every night for seventeen years.

But that night was different. His bed was empty, but the closet door was open and there he hovered, feet inches from the ground. He took his own life away because the people around him couldn't accept the way he lived it.

He was gay and not confused nor ashamed of or about it. He was a proud and confident young man who was extremely talented, both as a dancer and friend. His sexuality did not represent him, nor did he represent it. It was just a part of who he was.

People who didn't know the first thing about him verbally tortured him. Not only did they drive him to take his own life, but also killed something that I never thought would disappear; his spirit.

Words of ignorance collapsed onto his shoulders and pushed his passion for life through the ground.

I miss him every single day, but I know if he were still here today, he would tell me one thing; never stop dancing.

By Molly Morrison

CHAPTER 8
LOSS OF A MOTHER AND A COUSIN

Losing someone close to you is never easy. This is regardless of whether it's a long drawn out process, or sudden and unexpected. In my case, I lost two people in less than twelve months.

The first loss was my mom. She fought lung cancer for two long years. It is hard to say what was more difficult; learning for the first time she had a terminal illness, experiencing and watching her battle with treatments, or her actual death.

When my family first learned she had lung cancer, we were shocked, stunned, and maybe even surprised. My mom was a nurse for over 30 plus years. She was heavily devoted to community service. She co-created a community health clinic serving under-privileged areas. She was a devout Catholic, even contributing heavily to the building of a new church in my parents' neighborhood.

Because of all of this, we all could not understand how such an insidious disease could take over her body. What got me through this was when my mom finally lost her battle with cancer, the outpouring of support and accolades from her friends, colleagues and even other extended family was overwhelming.   There is a saying that "we never appreciate something until it's gone." That saying was never more accurate for me until my mother's actual death.

The weeks and months following her death and funeral, brought out stories of her generosity, love for life and passion for servicing others. Although I was still grieving it brought me peace to learn what an impact my mom made in other people's lives. As her son, things I took for granted growing up now seemed very relevant. I felt very fortunate to have been, unknowingly, on the receiving end of her generosity and thoughtfulness.

While I miss her dearly, I now feel a sense of pride (and pressure) to uphold her legacy and to pass on her stories to her grandchildren.

The second loss was a cousin that I also considered a younger brother. He was 37 years old. Unfortunately, while we were still dealing with the death of my mother, only nine months earlier, his death was sudden and unexpected. To make matters worse, his death happened only days leading up to Christmas day.

This particular holiday season was already going to be difficult as it was going to be the first without my mom, but then to lose another close family member made it especially hard. It's hard to say specifically how I made it through this period. Maybe I was still numb from dealing with my mom's death, or I was now experienced with dealing with the grieving process.

One thing is for certain, mourning with others seemed to be therapeutic. My cousin's sudden death brought back people (e.g., old friends, acquaintances, etc.) I had not seen in years. His death also reminded me that, "Life is about the Journey, and not the Destination."

While my cousin had many more dreams and goals to obtain, I am satisfied to know he fully enjoyed the journey, and died trying to get to his destination. While his death was a shock to everyone, it definitely reminded all of us that life is short. While we can get caught up in our daily lives, it is equally important to remember who and what things are important.

Losing someone that is close to you is difficult. Frankly, it's an experience I do not wish on anyone. However, we all will go through it at some point in our lives. I suggest instead of dwelling on how your loved one died, I say enjoy how they lived.

Remember the positive times and stories that you shared together. Remember their hopes and dreams, their accomplishments, and maybe the innocence you shared together.   The grieving process will bring out the worst in you, but it will also bring out the best. Try to embrace it as best you can.

Sincerely,
    Dean M Torres

CHAPTER 9
LOSS OF A HUSBAND

On the death of John
November 11, 1950 – March 20, 2004

My husband John was 48 years old when he became ill. There were a myriad of symptoms that didn't point to any particular illness. During the summer of 1999, in addition to his internist, we visited several medical specialists for; neuromuscular disease, infectious disease, a hematologist for bone marrow studies, a pulmonologist and urologist.   He also had an assortment of CT scans, MRI's and countless blood tests. He started calling it the "summer of medical testing".

By his choice, I accompanied John for every visit and test. I actually feel that being a part of the whole process was very important for two reasons: first, it made John more comfortable; and, second, I cannot overemphasize how important it is for every patient to have an advocate for their care.

It is a second pair of ears to hear what is said and remember it for further discussion. It is another vantage point from which information can be garnered for the well being of the patient.

My experience is that the sicker the patient, the more potentially important input may slip through the cracks. The end result of all these tests and examinations were that he appeared to have an unnamed autoimmune disease that caused him to lose approximately two thirds of his muscle mass, which resulted in significant joint and body pain.

In the last 18 months of his life, it also caused considerable changes in his thought processes. He was aware of these changes and that was one of the most difficult aspects of his illness with which to cope.

John was sick for five years. The progress of the illness was slow and debilitating. John was over 6'3" and normally weighed about 225 pounds. As his condition deteriorated, his weight plummeted to 140 pounds.

During those five years, he was hospitalized twice, taken to the emergency room twice with seizures.

There were two occasions when I was told that he would not survive his hospitalization and that I should alert our family and friends.

True to John's style, he proved the doctors wrong. I have never known anyone who had a stronger will. I have no doubt in my mind that he willed himself to continue to live until he had witnessed our oldest son graduate college and saw our two younger children graduate high school and start college.

We celebrated our 25th wedding anniversary just three months before he passed away. He was at home when he died and that was where he wanted and deserved to be.

How did John's illness and death affect our family and me? For me it brought into much sharper focus the idea that if there is an issue facing you and it is not a life or death situation, it is simply not important. Anything else can be fixed, solved or can wait for another time.

Friends have said to me that they didn't know how I could possibly manage to do all the things that I had to do and take care of John on a daily basis. Our children needed me and the household affairs still needed to be looked after, but for me it was simply a matter of priorities.

People are more important than things. Sick people need extra time and assistance. It was a very difficult balancing act and there are so many events and issues that took place that I don't really recall with clarity.

In January 2003, a little more than a year before John passed away, we faced another trial. Our oldest son was helping drive our daughter home from college when a vehicle driving on the wrong side of the highway ran their vehicle off the road. Amazingly, our daughter sustained only minor scrapes and bruises along with considerable emotional trauma. Our son was seriously injured with a severe head injury that left him in a coma for three weeks. He fully recovered and I view that as nothing short of a miracle.

The stress of that event contributed to John's second hospitalization, which lasted several weeks. I found myself waking very early each day so that I could begin my daily trek between two hospitals. It was without question the hardest thing that I have ever lived through.   I simply tried to do the very best that I could everyday with the information that I had at hand. I don't think that anyone can do more than to simply try to do their best.

Events and needs shift everyday. I know within the depths of my soul that the boundless love and prayers that were directed to my family were what made the difference at that time.

Coping was made easier because the process of the illness was slow and gradual. While there were times that I could not see any light at the end of the tunnel, somehow it was manageable because the worry increased in such a measured way that it kept me from realizing how enormous the pressure was becoming.

Ignorance is bliss. The few times that I had a break in the routine and I was suddenly aware of how "normal" everything could be, it made going back into my role as care giver almost unbearable. For me it was as simple as this; John was my husband and my best friend, and I could not and would not think of doing anything less for him.

One thing that I am very clear about is that I have no regrets. I feel that I was very lucky to have been able to talk with John about anything and everything before he passed away. I wish that John had been able to have those kinds of conversations with our children.

I am struck by the fact that at this point in my life I am very fortunate to still have my father alive and well and a part of my life.

John was with me for nearly half of my life. My children knew their father for what will be such a short part of their lives. I treasure how often I am able to talk to my father and ask him questions and learn from his maturity and wisdom. I wish that my children were able to do the same with their father. I wish that they could have had the opportunity to know him and talk to him with an adult's perspective. John and the children would have grown from those exchanges.

Life moves forward whether or not we feel that we are ready for it. That is probably a good thing. The pain and the sadness become easier to bear and life seems to return to some sort of normalcy. Time does help to heal our wounds and happiness continues.

I am eagerly anticipating the October wedding of our eldest son. In April, I was thrilled with the engagement of our second son, followed a few days later by our daughter. They have all found wonderful people with whom to share their lives and the circle of life continues!

During John's illness I came across a quote attributed to Mother Theresa. "I know God won't give me anything I can't handle, I just wish he didn't trust me so much." I still carry it with me everyday.

By Mary-Kay
    May, 2010

CHAPTER 10
MISCARRIAGE - LETTING GO

There he was, dark hair, dark eyes, dressed in his adorable jeans rolled up at the ankle and a short sleeve polo shirt. His hair had some gel to spike his bangs and the color of skin was mocha. Certainly, he wasn't a day older than three.

As I watched him from a distance I noticed a look of worry approaching his face.

Immediately he cried out, "Where's my mommy?"

As I looked around I noticed no one was responding to his frightened cry, so I ran over to the little boy.

"Are you okay little boy? Do you see your mommy?"

The little guy looked up at me with a big smile and said, "You're my mommy!"

I found myself sitting straight up in bed looking around my bedroom. The clock read 3:30 a.m. and it was still dark. My heart was filled with warmth and a sense of knowing, knowing that once again I met my future son in my dreams. The same dream, the same boy, the same scenario.

Surely this was meant to be.

We tried for several years to get pregnant and my body wasn't responding. I was timing my ovulation, urinating on ovulation sticks, forcing my husband to perform several times within a few day period of time.

Surely this was meant to be.

Another year passed and we were referred to a fertility specialist. Procedures and surgeries were performed. Serious mood changes, one minute feeling great, the next yelling at anyone in my path.

Surely this was meant to be.

We decided to try another doctor, the best-recommended specialist, and we did. Another surgery was done with a new procedure.   I was administered shots and medications for several weeks each on alternating sides of my body. The shots created serious emotional turmoil and the horrific side effect of swelling. I swelled up to four pant sizes.

Surely this was meant to be.

The doctor was expecting to retrieve seventeen eggs and I only produced three. Our chances shot down to a ten percent chance of success.

"We've made it this far let's keep going.

Two eggs died and one survived the fertilization of becoming an embryo. There he was, my little guy, my dream.

Surely this was meant to be.

The procedure was a success! My dream had come true and we were on our way to preparing for my little mocha skinned baby boy.

Surely this was meant to be.

Later, the Doctor called and with regret said the embryo had not successfully implanted. Was this meant to be? I am the only person that can answer this question.

I was in California with my family for Christmas when my doctor called. My husband chose to fly out at a later date due to work. The second I hung up the phone with my doctor I looked at my mother and brother and screamed, "I'm done! I'm done with my life, my husband, my marriage, my living in Georgia, and my career! This is not how I envisioned my life."

My husband flew in and I picked him up alone and told him everything the doctor had said and his response was complete silence. I felt as though I had done something wrong and that the miscarriage was somehow my fault.

Needless to say, the holidays were quite depressing for me. I told my husband several times before flying back to Georgia that I wasn't ready to go back home and maybe I needed some time alone with my family to help me get back on my feet emotionally. Of course, he disagreed and insisted upon my return.

To say the least I was extremely depressed. I barely made it to work and felt as if I functioned like a robot. Several women in the south sent me lovely cards and gifts and every card read, "Have faith Elena. This was meant to be. Everything happens for a reason. *This is God's will."*

If another woman told me, "Things in life happen for a reason" I swore I would have to slap them. This made me furious and even more depressed. How could God wish this for me? What have I done to deserve this? Why had God turned his head and allowed such a devastating experience happen to me?

Several months went by and I had my best friend move me out of the house while my husband was on a hunting trip. I called him and told him that I had moved out and I wanted a divorce. I knew I no longer was in love with him and that I wanted out. My girlfriends kept telling me it was because of the miscarriage that caused my drastic decisions. I disagreed.

I immediately began preparing for the sale of my business and making arrangements to return home, back to California. Of course, my husband did everything he could to change my mind but at this point in our marriage there was nothing he could do. I knew who he was, who I was and that our marriage was failing. We married for all of the wrong reasons.

The more decisions I made to return home, the stronger I got. I still wasn't ready to accept that my miscarriage was God's will. That was a great volcano of anger that I wasn't ready to face.

Within six months I sold my business, was offered a job in San Diego, and nothing was stopping me!

By the end of that summer I was once again back home, this time to stay.

Several years later, I have slowly taken the time to deal with my anger, frustration, feelings of loneliness and inadequacy. I have watched both of my little sisters begin their families with two adorable sons. Watching their pregnancies appeared to renew my anger and started the questions of, "What about me? Have you forgotten about me again?"

Today, I get it. I completely understand why I miscarried. Had I birthed that child I would literally be stuck living in Georgia. I would be living in a state which is not my home, dealing with an ex-husband and his family and raising a child as a single woman with no family around to help me.

Currently, I am still single, no husband, no baby, and I have never been happier with my life. Several years have passed since I had dreams of my sweet mocha baby boy. I would be lying if I said that I don't think of him because I do.

My sense of peace, sense of serenity and a sense of knowing that everything has turned out just the way it's supposed to has been God's gift to me. A gift that He never forgot about me, He never turned his head, He knew exactly what was to happen. It took me getting out of His way, letting go and learning to observe how my life has blossomed.

Surely this was meant to be!

By Elena Mendoza

CHAPTER 11
MEMORY BEARS

"If you learn from your suffering, and really come to understand the lesson you were taught, you might be able to help someone else who's now in the phase you may have just completed. Maybe that's what it's all about after all."

-Anonymous

I lost my husband, Eric, in a motorcycle accident on August 30, 2008. Eric had been participating in a large Christian biker event in Texas at the time, "Thunder Over Texas". He was traveling alone down a largely deserted open highway when a vehicle coming from the opposite direction made a left turn in front of him without looking into oncoming traffic. It is believed he was killed instantly.

As a devout Christian, my faith has sustained me during this storm in my life. A couple of months after Eric died, a friend of mine told me about her sister-in-law in New York who makes bears from a deceased loved ones article of clothing. I thought it was a wonderful idea and went to my husband's closet because I thought his family would love bears made from his clothes.

My husband loved a few things in his life. He loved God, he loved his Harley, he loved his family and friends, he loved food, and believe it or not, he loved shopping for clothes. Upon opening his closet, I found a plethora of choices for potential bear fabric. I was standing there, calculating how many shirts I would need and who would get what, when a thought struck me. Not only do I know how to sew, but I am quite an accomplished seamstress!

I laughed at the time because until that very moment the thought hadn't occurred to me that I could actually make them myself! Grief is such an odd thing. Forgetfulness is very common. Forgetting everyday things was becoming the norm for me at that time, my constant companion.

The first article of clothing that I could muster the courage to cut apart was a coverall Eric occasionally wore at work. I actually hadn't ever seen him wear the coverall, so cutting it to bits wasn't difficult for me. And the bear was adorable.

Upon completing it, I re-visited the closet and found a suitable shirt. I muttered an apology towards heaven as I took a pair of scissors to the very nice shirt. I believe it was a Tommy Bahama and, in turn, created a priceless treasure.

And then I kept on sewing. With my eyes gazing upwards towards the ceiling, I offered apologies and began cutting and restoring life back into the by this time dust collecting garments.

After creating more than a dozen and a half bears (and not even making a dent in my husband's wardrobe), I told myself I had to stop. The completed bears now covered my sofa and loveseat. Our little boy bears, "our sons" as I liked to refer to them, were taking over our house.

It wasn't long until Christmas arrived and all the "boys" went to live at their new homes with Eric's family and friends. I then began work on my own bears, which sit on a shelf in my bedroom today.

My father-in-law once told me that he would hold his bear every single day and cry, missing his son. He passed away 16 months after Eric, but I know that prior to his passing it meant the world to him to have his bear sitting with him on the couch every day. It was a comfort to him.

I learned something about myself in the months following Eric's death. I learned that I am a very blessed woman, with a wonderful support system of caring friends.

I also learned that I needed to keep creating bears, a mission of sorts, and a call from the Almighty to help provide comfort to the heartbroken.

I believe that is what these bears provide, comfort. What would otherwise be an unseen garment hanging in a dusty, musty closet, or scrunched up in a drawer, or even worse, packed away somewhere in a box, instead became something to be touched, admired, or even held tightly and sobbed into.

I try to add personal touches to the bears whenever possible. Besides embroidering loved ones initials on the bear, I have also added small "props" like guitars, glasses, various pins, baby pacifier, and other things. My goal is to create a unique and special memory bear for each and every customer.

Memory Bears is a blessing. A true blessing for me to create, and a blessing for the recipient who has a lifelong keepsake. It is an honor to be trusted with treasured articles of clothing, and I do not take lightly the responsibility I have in creating the best quality product possible. Let the body grieve itself.

You don't think you'll live past it and you don't really. The person you were is gone. But the half of you that's still alive wakes up one day and takes over again.

By Susan Huddleston

www.memorybearsbysusan.com
email:memorybearsbysusan@yahoo.com

CHAPTER 12
LOSS OF A DAUGHTER

I woke up early on January 1, 2000, the first day of the new century, and crawled out of my cave (the name I have given to my bed). It had been an uneventful New Year's Eve, in bed by 10 p.m., pillow over my ears to block out the sounds of centennial celebrations in my neighborhood.

I had spent the past several years at the bottom of pain after my twenty-one-year-old daughter, Jenna, was killed in a bus accident while studying abroad. Her death and that of three other students on the bus in India had made news all around the world. And here I was, several years later, a heartsick father, convinced there was nothing further to celebrate, ever.

I had gone through the motions of trying to put my world back together, acting as if my life would one day have purpose and meaning again, secretly hoping this debilitating pain would subside, praying I would one day be reunited with my "angel daughter" and striving to be a good father to my surviving daughter, Stefie — but I was living under a cloud of despair. My life, as I had known it, had ended. There would be no good times, no celebrations, not without Jenna.

As I stepped out of bed over Rascal, my black lab, nestled in her spot bedside the bed, the phone rang. It was my friend Anne, in a panic and asking for my help. "Ken, I'm worried about Howard. He's been very depressed all week. Would you please call him, Ken? Today!'

And so it was that I called my buddy Howard, whose third-generation family business was losing millions of dollars and facing a hostile takeover.

Howard was glad to hear from me.

In response to my invitation to "go to lunch," he said, "I'm on my way to yoga. Why don't you join me and we can go for lunch afterwards?"

Realizing I could help a friend in trouble and escape my own misery for a few hours, I agreed and scrambled around for some sneakers and shorts. I wasn't quite sure what people wore to a yoga class.

An hour later, I was sitting lotus style on a yoga mat next to Howard in a room full of bright-eyed yoga students. A surprising number of them were men my age that appeared to be in pretty good shape, and I began to wonder what I had gotten myself into. I could not remember the last time I had stretched a muscle; I'd also been filling the sadness and emptiness of each day with food since Jenna's death and had gained twenty-five pounds.

Sitting there among a group of straight-backed, New Age yoga types who obviously knew what they were doing, I felt terribly out of place. And then I gazed over at my friend, Howard, his face full of anguish, and smiled. He looked back at me, trying to smile and I was quickly reminded why I was there. I felt somehow closer to Howard than ever before, like he was beginning to understand what it was like to have you heart ripped out.

As the class settled in, a beautiful, soft-spoken yoga teacher named Diane invited us to turn our attention inward. She asked us to*"find a comfortable position,*
> *close your eyes.*
> *Take a deep breath in,*
> *and on the out breath,*
> *release any tension*
> *you might be holding."*

Weaving a bare-foot path through the mire of 25 students who had gathered for her class that morning, Diane spoke the first of many words I would never forget.

"Take a deep breath and let go! Let the body breathe itself." What? I thought.

My breathing had become shallow and controlled. My pain was often so big; I did not know whether I could make it to the next moment. I had been holding on, fighting just to survive. And yet, listening to Diane's soft, reassuring voice, I was able to surrender a little bit at a time.

"Let the body breathe itself," I repeated over and over until I could feel myself soften and then let go.

My body had been frozen by the trauma of my daughter's death. Each cell had been turned inside out. In a way, I too had died, had ceased to breathe. But here I was sitting on a yoga mat, discovering new breath, new movement and new life.

Diane then led us into yoga posture she called "the heart opener."

Before I was able to fully grasp what was happening to me, I had let out a soft, harrowing sigh. Tears began running down my cheek.

In that moment, I had discovered a new cave, a safe, 5,000-year-old refuge for my grief called 'yoga.'

In the remaining 45 minutes of the class, Diane's soothing voice led me on a gentle journey back into my body, my heart and my soul.

The more she guided us, saying things like, "Let yourself in, gently, compassionately, without straining," the more I realized how I had locked myself out. I had shut down my body and emotions. Without really being aware of it, I was dying. Like many parents who experience the unspeakable, unthinkable nightmare of losing a child, I had shut down as a means of coping with the seemingly unending pain and put myself into a sort of coma.

Guided and encouraged by a wise and caring teacher, I took my first baby steps back into life. Yoga, I discovered, was really the practice of self-compassion and a path to begin healing my life. Yoga taught me to reopen my heart, take care of my body and quiet my mind. Diane's invitations to "notice how your body is different each day" and "differentiate between tension and strength" taught me more about healing after a loss and the rebirth of hope than any book I had read.

I began to find nourishment in silence and felt somehow more connected with Jenna in those moments. At the end of my first class, as we sat silently, I spoke silently to Jenna, telling her how much I loved her, that I was going to fight my way back into life and make her proud of me for not giving up. In the weeks and months to follow, I learned to calm my exhausted mind and to reactivate the "fight back" and "fell good" systems in my body. With good coaching, I learned that it was okay to allow grief to move through me. "Let the body grieve itself," became my mantra.

It became a ritual for me to gently place my hand over my heart and allow the tears flow for several moments during each class. I would talk to Jenna during the closing meditation. I was clearing the way for a new life, one in which I could live with and through my loss. I would always grieve the loss of my daughter.

Now I could experience the joy and privilege of having had her in my life for twenty-one precious years. She would be in my heart forever. Since that day, I have attended yoga classes two or three times a week. I am gradually learning to live in my own skin again. I now accept that grieving is as choice less as breathing. It cannot be forced or resisted, but it can be allowed. This, and the lesson of self-compassion, is taught every day to bereaved parents through the programs of The Jenna Druck Center (www.jennadruck.org).

As for me personally, I keep myself in top shape through yoga, physically, mentally and spiritually, and I honor both my daughter's by helping others find their way through the darkness that is grief.

I thought I was going to a New Year's Day yoga class to help a friend. And maybe I did. As it turns out, I was also saving my own life.

By Dr. Ken Druck

CHAPTER 13
LOSS OF A FATHER

The call came in around midnight. The nurse on the other end of the line said that I needed to come very soon. I asked her what was happening, and she said his color was changing. My heart sank. I told my twelve-year-old son that I had to go to the hospital, because grandpa was dying.

He said, "I can't go with you Mom. I can't watch Grandpa die." I told him I knew that, and I said I would call his older brother to come home and stay with him.

I called my son, Ben, and he was at a casino way on the other side of town with a friend. I told him to get home as quickly as possible. I really didn't want to leave my son, David, but I knew there was no choice. I ran upstairs to my room and sat on the edge of my bed and started crying quietly. I decided to give prayer a try, even though I don't really believe in God.

Through my tears, I said, "Please don't take my dad away from me. Please don't! Please don't take him away!"

I ran back downstairs and told David I had to go. He said "I'll be fine Mom. Go. Just go. You've got to go."

I drove to the hospital through a flood of tears. I parked and ran to the door that I had gone through too many times.

Of course, it was locked. I saw the call button and pushed it firmly. The nurse answered, "ICU". I told her I needed to get in to see my dad and gave her my name and his name. She said, "Okay, it will be a minute."

I waited and waited for what seemed like at least five minutes. Nothing.

I buzzed again, and said, "I have to get in to see my father!"

She said, "Oh, okay," and the main door opened. I ran to the ICU; my father had been in there for at least four days by this time. Another door with another buzzer! I hit the buzzer and gave yet another person my name and my father's name. This time the door unlocked very quickly.

I ran to the room that my dad was in. My sister was with him holding his hand. I tried to calm myself quickly. He was alive! I was happy that I had made it. He and my sister were talking quietly. The television was on. My Dad was saying that he wished he felt better, because it was the night Barack Obama was accepting the nomination as the candidate from the Democratic Party.

My Dad had always been a liberal Democrat. He grew up in San Antonio and had seen racial discrimination at its worst. The idea that a black man was going to run for president was amazing to him.

I told him that I had stopped by earlier in the day with flowers and a card, but he was sleeping. He said he was wondering how the card and flowers had been put there.

He explained to us that he had been really tired the past couple of days and his back was bothering him a lot. I figured the cancer had spread into his kidneys.

We talked for a little while longer, and then he said the words I will never forget, "Come here girls and give me a hug". My sister and I did and then we began to cry softly. It was difficult to keep myself from falling apart, but I wanted to be strong for him. I could see that he had finally accepted that he was going to die. It was hard for me to believe it, because he had fought so hard to live for many years. He loved life so much!

One week earlier, he opened his eyes in the Urgent Care of the same hospital and smiled and said, "It's a beautiful day! You are all here with me! This is wonderful!"

My sister, Jane, my son, Ben, and my brother's son, Josh, and I looked at each other in amazement.

Josh chuckled, and said, "But Grandpa, you're in the emergency room of a hospital".

My dad said, "But I am still here!" As this awful night progressed, Ben and Josh arrived at the hospital. Ben told me that his good friend, Joe, would stay with David, so I didn't need to worry.

Josh had called my brother in Belgium, so he would be able hear what was going on; my father was not able, at that point, to speak to my brother on the phone. I felt terrible for my brother to have to hear all of this on a cell-phone.

The morphine was taking effect by now and my dad was not conscious anymore. We all took turns hugging and kissing him and telling him how much we loved him.

My son, Ben, hugged me for a long time which was extremely comforting. In a way, the fact that he was with me, helped create a bridge to the future. This night was one of the most difficult I had ever experienced.

After he passed away, I was in shock. It broke my heart that cancer had taken him away from me and that he missed seeing his first great-grandchild by nine days. He was so looking forward to meeting her. I was relieved that my sister and I had succeeded in keeping him out of the enormous pain that his sister had suffered from the same type of cancer thirty-seven years earlier. He had told us that he'd had a wonderful life and that he had been able to do a lot of things that most people could only dream about.

It has been three years now, and I miss him terribly. I try to remind myself daily about my dad's perpetual optimism and tremendous courage.

I know he would say, "Laura, I am fine. Don't worry about me. Enjoy your life, because it goes by quickly".

By Laura Salik

CHAPTER 14
LOSS OF A CHILD

*"Although the world is full of suffering,
it is full also of the overcoming of it."*

-Helen Keller

When I was six months pregnant, I found out the devastating news that my baby had a lethal bone condition called Ontogenesis ImperfectaType 2.

I was told that if I was lucky enough to make it to term that my child was not healthy enough to sustain life on his own and would most likely die shortly after birth.

My sweet little baby, George, was born on April 11, 1999, and died just 15 minutes later. As much as I knew death was his most likely outcome, nothing can prepare you for what it's like when it actually occurs.

Luckily, I had wonderful nurses and doctors, and the rest of the great staff who treated my baby, me and my family with such dignity, loving care and kindness that it make the whole situation much less painful.

Along with the tremendous emotional pain I was feeling after baby George died, I was experiencing some surprising physical symptoms as well. First, my heart hurt, I mean it literally ached. I felt like I had an open wound in my chest and the only way I felt better was to hold my hand on my heart and apply pressure.

The second pain I had was an aching in my arms. I was completely surprised by this and had no idea why they would hurt so much. It wasn't until a week later when I picked up a large ceramic pot that weighed about five or six pounds did I realize what the pain could be. My arms where aching to hold a new baby.

When I held an object that was about the right size in circumference and weight of a baby, my aching went away. I have since read that these two physical pains can be a common response after the loss of a baby.

That's when I had the idea to create "the Comfort Cub" a weighted teddy bear for a mother who has lost a baby to hold when her arms hurt and her heart is aching. Each Comfort Cub comes with a handwritten note that reads:

Dear friend, I am so very sorry for your loss. I too lost my precious baby. My heart hurt so much and my arms felt so empty. I know no words can be spoken or gifts given that can take away the deep pain you may be feeling. My hope in sending you this bear is that in some small way it will bring a little bit of comfort to your arms. With love, a fellow mom.

Since the time I created The Comfort Cub, over ten years ago, the bear is now being used in many different ways. It is no longer just being used for mothers who have lost a baby, but it has been found to be comforting for anyone in grief.

This therapeutic teddy bear has been used to help with the loss of any loved ones or to heal a heart broken for any reason.

I was surprised to learn it even helped to bring comfort to an entire high school football team after the loss of their teammate. One mom shared with me that her teenage son slept with it every night. In fact, this is the number one comment I have received about the bear, that it helps people to sleep more soundly at night. Anyone who has suffered a loss knows how very hard it can be to sleep at night.

If you are in grief, or you know of someone who is, you can get a free Comfort Cub by contacting San Diego Hospice at 619-688-1600 or at www.thecomfortcub.com.

My hope is that this special little bear will help to bring you some love and comfort too.

By Marcella Johnson

CHAPTER 15
LOSS OF A MOTHER

"If you're going through hell, keep going."

-Winston Churchill

Grief.
It's all consuming.
It's overwhelming.
It's inescapable.
t's indescribable.
It's just the worst thing possible.

When you love someone with every fiber of your being, then lose them to cancer, a ridiculously unfair disease that sneaks up and steals your life, it's as if you've lost a part of yourself. And it's something that you can never ever get back. To love so deeply and then lose that love…is outrageously horrific.

She was my Mom. She was my closest and dearest friend. She was my person. Her loss devastated me. And it changed who I am. I will never be the same without her. She was my world. And I was hers. And now I am drifting through life without her. It's like trying to catch the wind with a hole in your sail.

Stories of Loss and Survivial

It's been several years since my Mom passed and I still ache every single day. Why can't I see the big picture? That this is the circle of life. That I have a husband and children who need me. That she'd want me to be happy and not consumed with grief. Why can't I grasp that concept?

I have friends and family who were and are supportive on the rare occasions Ilet them see me grieving. But most have not lost a parent or don't have the relationship I had with my Mom. Not to mention that I lost my father, too, when I was a teenager. So now I don't have anyone "above" me…I'm at the top now and it's a lonely place to be. Most friends can't comprehend the depth of my grief, and honestly, I don't need them to and certainly don't wish it upon any of them.

A few weeks after the loss they had moved on and I was (and am) still stuck in this sad, sad empty world without her. I'm sure they think, "why is she still so sad?" "Why can't she move on?" I don't know.

Is there truly a time limit on grief? I don't think so. Until you live it you really can't judge it. Grief is personal; it's independent of rules, time frames, expectations. I know that everyone handles it differently. My one brother seems to stifle it. I'm not sure how he handles it in the very private places in his life, but I have yet to see him shed a tear or truly emote. He doesn't handle my tears well at all. My other brother is just sad and misses our Mom as much as I do, but his world is completely different than mine so his depth of depression far exceeds mine. No one can predict how grief will affect him or her; it is elusive and unpredictable...but very real and extremely painful.

But therapy is good. Your friends get tired of listening to your sadness and grief. The whole consoling thing gets old and can put a strain on any friendship or relationship. So therapy works. My therapist listens, advises and helps as I talk, weep and grieve. Instead of ruining relationships, a therapist must listen to the monotony of my sad life, because that's why I pay the fee, for someone to listen and console. I recommend therapy to everyone who grieves.

So as I put on a happy face every day for my family, friends and acquaintances just so I can exist through the day, I am always suppressing a gut-wrenching ache, a need to sob uncontrollably and scream from the rooftops that I love you, need you and miss you Mom. I want everyone whose life she touched to think about her and not forget how absolutely wonderful she was. How she lit up a room, lent a ear to a friend, consoled those who were in need, gave generously to the needy, entertained magnificently, and was a compassionate, unselfish, caring and giving friend. I think that worries me that people will forget. But I never will. Ever.

Stories of Loss and Survivial

But just so you know, I don't wallow in self-pity on a daily basis. I don't appear sad or depressed. I am enjoying my family and friends and continuing to live a happy life. My parents would want that. I want that. And I have fun, laugh and love all the time. Life is good; it's all about keeping grief personal and in its place. I'm a work in progress, but I think I'm doing pretty well.

And writing this has been very cathartic. It's what my therapist has wanted me to do, to journal, to write things down. I haven't been able to until now. So glad I wrote this. It helps.

By Lauren Selwyn Sommer

Michelle Oleff Cohn

SUGGESTIONS

While researching this book, I have talked with many people, counselors, religious leaders, and read articles on what one can do to help survive during this time. While there is no one perfect answer, I have put together recommendations that most people have said has helped in some way.

I wish I had a cure, a definite answer, a magical power to take the pain away, but I don't. What I can give you are the suggestions and thoughts from others who have been through a loss and found the strength to go on.

~Breathe- As simple as this sounds, it really can make a difference. It's something you have complete control over, and you can do it anywhere. When you're feeling overwhelmed, take a few very deep breaths, inhale deeply, hold your breath for a few seconds, and then let it out. People don't tend to practice this on their own and it is a powerful tool to assist in reducing stress. Sometimes it's all you can do to survive. When all else fails, just focus on one breath at a time.

~Be true to your feelings - If you feel as though you can't get out of bed, don't. You don't have to push yourself into something your not ready for. Everyone heals at different times and in different ways. Only **YOU** know what's best for you. There may be days you just can't face the world and that's okay. Don't do it until you're ready. When people have major surgery, they stay in a hospital and have round-the-clock care to help with their recovery. They are required to do so by the doctor, and pushing themselves can make things worse in the long run. **YOU** have been through a major break in your heart. You need to take the time to recover. Your heart will never heal back exactly as it used to be, but it will begin to heal in a new way. Allow yourself the time. Don't expect quick results, rather expect to take the time your heart needs.

~Get out- When you are ready, find some sort of physical activity that you like. It might be a bike ride, Yoga class, sporting activities, a run, a walk, and countless others. Something to get your blood flowing. Whether you have an hour or 15 minutes, every little bit can help. I once talked with a woman who suddenly lost her husband. She told me that one of the most essential activities that helped her survive the grief was a morning walk with her neighbor. She made a commitment to walk with her each morning, and sometimes that was the only reason she got out of bed. She didn't always want to do it, but she always felt better after she did.

~Write- Write your thoughts down. This is a good tool during those times when you can't turn your brain off or when you may feel like you have exhausted all of your friends with your thoughts. You may feel as though you don't want to say your thoughts out loud. Write all your feelings down. It doesn't have to be in any particular order or form. It can be a list of feelings, a memory, a thought, or something you just don't want to say out loud. It's just a place for you to get your thoughts and feelings out. A place to go anytime, day or night, and it will never judge you or how you feel.

~Allow people to help you- Sometimes it's hard to accept help from family and friends. The fact is that sooner or later we all need help in some way. If people want to be there for you, let them. It's okay to let people in when you need help and support. Cry with a friend. Plan to get out of the house. Plan to go out to eat. Share your feelings. Chances are that someday those same people will need your help and support.

~Find a Counselor who specializes in grief recovery, and/or a support group - You might get to the point that you feel you have exhausted your friends with your grief. They may not understand what you're going through and don't know how to help you. A grief counselor has been trained to help with what you're going through. They will have the education and resources to assist you through the recovery process.

~Take time for yourself - You might want to be alone sometimes and that's okay. Sometimes having too many people around can be overwhelming. If you need time to yourself, don't be afraid to tell people. This is a time that you need to take care of yourself. It is important to pay attention to eating healthy, getting the sleep you need, and not letting yourself get run down. Be kind to yourself.

~Cry if you need to- Don't be afraid to cry. It's a way of releasing tension and sadness. Allow yourself to feel and grieve. Crying is a healthy outlet of relieving your body's stress. Allow it to happen when you need to. Find a safe place, and let it out. I have talked with people who have said they just wanted to scream. One man told me, he went to the beach and screamed at the ocean. Another woman told me that she got into her car and just yelled and hit the steering wheel. Sometimes you might need to let your emotions out in a safe environment.

~Take notice of the beauty around you-
Take time to smell the flowers, watch the sun rise or set, and look at the trees and sky. Try to notice and appreciate nature. Find your own peace in nature.

~Volunteer with an organization you believe in- You might not have the strength right now, but when your feeling up to trying new things, helping others can make you feel better. You don't have to commit long term. You can try something for a couple hours to see how it makes you feel. It may help you get your mind off things for awhile.

~Try to live one day at a time- or even moment-to-moment. All you can do is your best to make it through each day. Don't have expectations of when you should feel better. There is no way to predict that feeling. Rather appreciate each time you do have a good moment, hour, day, and eventually week and month.

~Make plans to do an activity you enjoy-
Here are some suggestions:
Exercise
Plans with a friend
Go out to a nice dinner
Meet a friend for coffee
Watch a movie (keep it light)
Get a massage
Call a friend
(or e-mail if you're not up for talking)
Watch a sporting event
Play or join a sport team
Listen to music

Sleep in

Read a book or magazine

*Take up something you've been
  meaning to do, but have put it off.*

Take a long bath

Meditation

* Learn something new*

Do something for someone else

Acupuncture

Learn about vitamins and supplements

*Remember what you used to enjoy and make
time to do it.*

All these ideas are not cures and; unfortunately, they won't make your pain go away. What these ideas do is get you on the road back to living. A baby doesn't learn how to walk in a day. It takes time learning how to sit on its own, then even more time learning how to crawl, and eventually, with time and practice, the baby learns how to walk forward.

This may be a long process for you to figure out how to get your strength to walk again. Don't expect it to happen right away.

You need to allow yourself the time to go at your own pace. Don't try to rush recovery. Some days are going to be extremely difficult. Allow yourself to have the bad days. Those are the days you just breathe one breath at a time. Tomorrow might be better.

Michelle Oleff Cohn

WEBSITES AND BOOKS

http://www.thrivingalifecrisis.com
Title: *How to Thrive Not Just Survive a Life Crisis.*

http://www.secretstoemotionalhealth
Title: *Online Personal Growth Program for Health, Wealth and Happiness.*

http://www.compassionatefriends.org
Title: *The Compassionate Friends/USA*

http://www.jennadruck.org
Title: Ken Druck,Ph.D., *Healing Your Life After the Loss of a loved one and How to Talk to Your Kids about Violence.*
(Founder, The Jenna Druck Foundation & Families Helping Families program).

Ken Druck, Ph.D., *The Secrets Men Keep: Find Out What They Think....How They Really Feel* (Ballantine Books, 1987).

Elizabeth Edwards, *Resilience-Reflections on the Burdens and Gifts Facing Life's Adversities* (Broadway).

Noel, Brook & Blair, Ph.D.,Pamela D., *I Wasn't Ready to Say Goodbye*

Cross,MS,MFT, Darlene F., *A New Normal-Learning to Live With Grief and Loss* (Darlene Cross 2010).

http://www.robertzucker.com
Zucker, Robert, *The Journey Through Grief and Loss: Helping Yourself and Your Child When Grief*

Stories of Loss and Survivial Is Shared (St.Martin's Press, 2009).

John W. James and Russell Friedman, T*he Grief Recovery Handbook and Moving On* (Harper Collins).

Matthews, Ph.D., Leslie Landon, *When Children Grieve,* (Harper Collins)

Evans, M., *Moving On*

Canfield, Jack and Hansen, Mark Victor, *Chicken Soup For The Grieving Soul*
(Health Communications, Inc., 2003 Deerfield Beach, FL)

Canfield, Jack, Hansen, Mark Victor, and Newmark, Amy, *Chicken Soup for the Soul:,Grieving and Recovery*
(Chicken Soup for the Soul Publishing, LLC, 2011).

Glanz, Barbara A., *What Can I Do? Ideas to Help Those Who Have Experienced Loss*
(Augsburg Books, 2007)

Schwiebert, Pat and Deklyen, *Chuck, Tear Soup A Recipe For Healing After Loss*
(Grief Watch Portland, Oregon USA, 2004)

http://www.tearsoup.com
Doka, Kenneth J. & Martin, Terry L., *Grieving Beyond Gender: Understanding the Ways Men and Women Mourn*
(New York: Routledge, 2010)

http:// www.aplb@aplb.org
The Association for Pet Loss and Bereavement

Bereavement and Beyond
Video designed to support those dealing with the death of a loved one. Interviews and analysis show how people cope and deal with loss and bereavement.
http://www.bereavementandbeyond.com

Compassion Connection
Offering comfort and hope to those grieving loss of child, spouse, parents, siblings, missing, suicide, tragedy, divorce, abused. Loss of health, loss of pet, loss of job. Processing grief. Inspirational.
http://www.compassionconnection.org

GriefNet
Support services include resource referral, support groups, a library, and memorial web pages. Links to Suicide Prevention and Survivors' Resources. Rivendell Resources, a charitable corporation.
http://griefnet.org

Death and Dying from About.com
Links for the grieving widow, widower, child, teen and adult. Dedicated to the bereaved, the dying and those who care for them. Includes all issues about dying, pet loss, and memorials.
http://dying.about.com

Grieving the Loss of a Parent
Alexandra Kennedy.com, seven tasks and ten steps of recovery, supporting a friend, books, tapes, workshops, and articles.
http://www.alexandrakennedy.com

Grief and Renewal

International site to support people in their journeys of recovery and rebuilding following a loss. Resources, links, bulletin board, and people's stories of renewal.

http://www.griefandrenewal.com

http:// www.griefsteps.com Many resources to help with books, online support, support groups and more.

Journey of Hearts

A healing place in cyberspace created by a physician who combines medicine, psychiatry, poetry, prose and images to provide resources and support.

http://www.journeyofhearts.org

A Time to Grieve

Explores the experience of grief after the loss of a parent and offers support, simple suggestions, and a place for sharing memories.

http://atimetogrieve.net

The Comfort Zone

Writings of comfort and inspiration for those who grieve.

http://www.meyna.com/comfzone.html

GriefWeb

A collection of literature and links to help you cope with the loss of a loved one.

http://www.geocities.com/griefweb

GriefLossRecovery.com
Articles, memorials, poetry, and provides a safe haven for bereaved persons to share their grief through discussion forums.
http://www.grieflossrecovery.com

GriefLink
Information resource on death related grief for the community and professionals. Includes coping with grief, helping the bereaved, resources, education, and specific topics.
http://www.grieflink.asn.au

The Rainbow
Hope, inspiration, and encouragement in the form of essays, photos and poems for anyone going through grief recovery.
http://www.geocities.com/fernalea/index.html

Healing Grief
Spiritual resources for people in grief. Invitations to contribute stories about after-death communication, miracles, inspirations, mystical photos. Includes a healing journey, bookstore, tapes, and consultations, created by a widow to share with other people in grief.
http://www.healgrief.com

http://www.aarp.org/families
AARP offers a wide variety of resources and information for the bereaved.

http://www.americanhospice.org/griefzone
An educational resource for employers, educators, healthcare providers, and others on matters of death and loss.

http://www.centering.org

The Centering Corporation is a non-profit organization dedicated to providing education and resources for the bereaved. It has an extensive catalogue of grief resources, including books, workbooks and memory items for sale.

http://www.thecompassionatefriends.org

The Compassionate Friends is a national nonprofit, self-help support organization that offers friendship, understanding, and hope to bereaved parents, grandparents and siblings.

http://www.griefnet.org

Griefnet is an Internet community of persons dealing with loss and grief.

http://www.hospicefoundation.org

Comprehensive website focusing on terminal illness, death, and grief.

LINKS TO MANY GRIEF-RELATED ARTICLES AND RESOURCES

Journey of Hearts
A healing place in cyberspace created by a physician who combines medicine, psychiatry, poetry, prose and images to provide resources and support.
http://www.journeyofhearts.org

http://www.seasonspress.com
A wealth of excellent articles by John Schneider, Ph.D., a clinical psychologist, author and nationally recognized expert in the transformative power of grief.

http://www.suicidology.org
See section devoted to information and resources for survivors. (those who have lost a loved one to suicide).

http://www.widownet.org
WidowNet is an information and self-help resource for and by people who have lost a life partner.

Notes and Thoughts '

Notes and Thoughts

Michelle Oleff Cohen (pictured with a "Comfort Cub") graduated from San Diego State University with a degree in child development. She resides in San Diego with her two children, Dani and Maxx.

Michelle is a first-time author who was looking for a way to bring comfort and support to people who have suffered a devasting loss.

Her exploration through her contributors' stories, demonstrates how one can cope and survive when all hope is gone.

www.ingramcontent.com/pod-product-compliance
Lightning Source LLC
Chambersburg PA
CBHW070906280326
41934CB00008B/1609